A Book of American Trade-Marks & Devices

Also from Westphalia Press
westphaliapress.org

A Book of American Trade-Marks & Devices

An Illustration of Early Advertising Logos

By Joseph Sinel

WESTPHALIA PRESS
An Imprint of Policy Studies Organization

Westphalia Press
An imprint of Policy Studies Organization
1527 New Hampshire Ave., NW
Washington, D.C. 20036
info@ipsonet.org

ISBN-13: 978-1-63391-268-7
ISBN-10: 1-63391-268-X

Cover design by Jeffrey Barnes:
jbarnesbook.design

Daniel Gutierrez-Sandoval, Executive Director
PSO and Westphalia Press

Updated material and comments on this edition
can be found at the Westphalia Press website:
www.westphaliapress.org

A BOOK OF
AMERICAN
TRADE-MARKS
& DEVICES

COMPILED BY

JOSEPH SINEL

NEW YORK
ALFRED·A·KNOPF
1924

INTRODUCTION

❧ A search on our library shelves reveals an amazing mass of data concerning the trade-mark, practically all of which treats of the legal side of the subject, while such an important feature as design is ignored almost entirely. ❧ Always it is the arrangement of form, the carefully conceived units of design that make the distinctive emblem or device that is to secure identity for that which it represents. ❧ A distinguishing mark is so increasingly important to a modern business that careful thought should be given the selection of its elements, and skill and taste exercised in the decorative treatment. A good trade-mark is frequently a gradual evolution. The trade-mark, often, influences the appearance of the product, the printed matter and much of the advertising of its owner. ❧ Simplicity is the keynote of a good mark. Whatever form is used should be so simple in elements and execution that its poster quality will establish a definite and sustained impression; a form that will not lose its essential features no matter how small it may be. ❧ Flexibility, the ready adjustment to new conditions or requirements is next in importance, in order that a mark may be executed in metals, fabrics, electric signs, transparencies and the like, in addition to being rendered in line, tone and various color schemes and sizes for many printing processes. ❧ A device or emblem is generally more impressive and individual when its form is not controlled by the circle, square, diamond, triangle or other such usual shapes. An irregular

3

shaped mark, determined by the object, registers a much quicker and more lasting impression. A reference to the Fisher Body mark and that of McCutcheon's will illustrate this point. The Fisher mark, beautiful as it is, would be more individual and distinctive if the rectangular frame were omitted. ❧ Of similar interest is the use of objects or abstract forms in preference to the usual trade names, firm names or slogans. Not only do these obtain better design arrangements, but they speak a universal language when used on goods destined for foreign countries where the American name or phrase would be practically meaningless. ❧ For the most part, our national advertisers use marks, that may have distinctive features, but which are frequently so devoid of design merit as to be positively ugly; consequently the majority of designs here reproduced are those of less well known organizations and individuals. ❧ Too many of our marks which possess uncommon merit are borrowed or adapted from European examples. Especially is this noticeable in those used by some of our printers and publishers. ❧ Noteworthy and delightful trade devices by such designers as W. A. Dwiggins, Harvey Hopkins Dunn, T. M. Cleland, C. B. Falls, Edward Penfield, René Clarke and others, relieve the dull level of the vast field of American trade marks. ❧ Whenever it has been possible to secure authentic information, the name of the designer has been given. Frequently, the idea for a trade-mark was suggested by one man and executed by several, or vice-versa. ❧ While this does not attempt to be a technical book on trade-mark designing, it does present a comprehensive range of contemporary design examples from the many thousands of available marks. Its purpose is to show marks that have ornamental significance as well as characteristic trade value, with the hope that it will prove a worthy influence in the creation of new marks and in the adaptation of old ones. ❧ The making of this book was possible only through the co-operation of designers and owners of the various marks. And although it would be impractical to attempt acknowledgment to each individual or group, special mention should be made of indebtedness to Mr. Alfred A. Knopf, and to Mr. Elmer Adler of the Pynson Printers. The generous assistance of the Beck Engraving Co., the Japan Paper Company and the E. C. Lewis Co. contributed much to the successful completion of the work. The compiler desires to express to all of these his grateful appreciation.

J.S.

HART SCHAFFNER & MARX

CHICAGO

FINIS · CORONAT · OPUS

THE JOHN S. KING COMPANY

CLEVELAND

THE NEW REPUBLIC

NEW YORK

ALEXANDER BROTHERS

PHILADELPHIA

Was soll ich damit tun?

THE WHITE ELEPHANT

HINGHAM CENTER, MASS.

9

FORBES LITHOGRAPH MFG. CO.

BOSTON

AMERICAN WRITING PAPER CO.

HOLYOKE, MASS.

CONDE NAST PUBLICATIONS

VOGUE

NEW YORK

ROGERS & COMPANY

NEW YORK

JAPAN PAPER COMPANY

NEW YORK

LA FAYETTE MOTORS CORPORATION

MILWAUKEE

B. W. HUEBSCH, INC.
NEW YORK

THE AMERICAN PRINTER

NEW YORK

TAYLOR & TAYLOR

SAN FRANCISCO

STRATHMORE PAPER COMPANY

MITTINEAGUE, MASS.

STRONG · TO · SERVE

HORNE AND LIVINGSTON

SAN FRANCISCO

THE THEATRE GUILD, INC.

NEW YORK

JAMES McCUTCHEON & COMPANY

NEW YORK

PYNSON PRINTERS INCORPORATED

NEW YORK

THE ARTISTS' GUILD OF THE AUTHORS'
LEAGUE OF AMERICA, INC.
NEW YORK

WILLS SAINTE CLAIRE, INC.

MARYSVILLE, MICH.

THE
AMBASSADOR
AND PUBLICITY DIGEST

NIAGARA PAPER MILLS

LOCKPORT, N.Y.

BODY
by
FISHER

FISHER BODY CORPORATION

DETROIT

27

THE WHITE COMPANY

CLEVELAND

CHEMICAL PAPER MANUFACTURING CO.

HOLYOKE, MASS.

F. G. BROWN & COMPANY

CHICAGO

TRE-JUR

UNITED TOILET GOODS COMPANY

NEW YORK

HARRY ST. JOHN DIXON

SAN FRANCISCO

.

ERWIN, WASEY & COMPANY, LTD.

CHICAGO

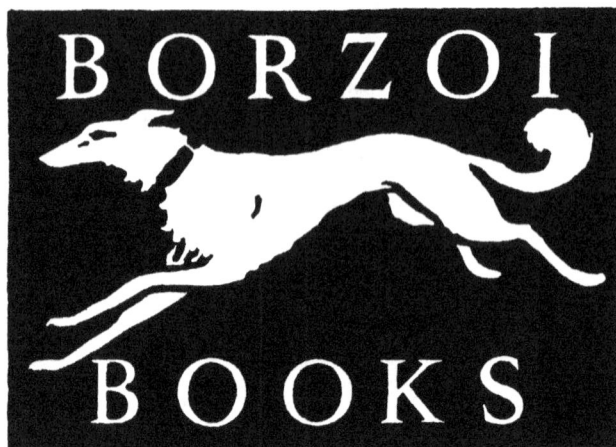

BORZOI BOOKS

ALFRED A. KNOPF, INC.
NEW YORK

C. H. MASLAND & SONS, INC.

PHILADELPHIA

U. S. TREASURY DEPARTMENT WAR SAVINGS STAMPS
WASHINGTON, D.C.

SUNWISE TURN INC.
NEW YORK

E. G. GALT
SAN FRANCISCO

THE DAM PUTERSCHEIN'S SONS
HINGHAM, MASS.

ALFRED BARTLETT
BOSTON

ADVERTISERS PAPER MILLS
HOLYOKE, MASS.

WINOLD REISS
DECORATING COMPANY
NEW YORK

A. B. KIRSCHBAUM COMPANY
PHILADELPHIA

FREDERICK GOETZE
NEW BRUNSWICK, N. J.

SANDHILL FRUIT GROWERS ASSOCIATION (INC.)
ABERDEEN, N. C.

WESTER BROS.
NEW YORK

HARRIS AUTOMATIC PRESS CO.
CLEVELAND

ROBERT JOHN KNOX GORE
DETROIT

STETSON SHOE CO., INC.
WEYMOUTH, MASS.

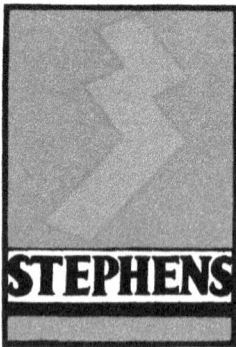

STEPHENS MOTOR CAR CO., INC.
MOLINE, ILL.

SUGAR PRODUCTS CO.
NEW YORK

NEW ERA SPRING &
SPECIALTY COMPANY
GRAND RAPIDS

38

BLUE MILL

PERRY W. BROWNING
WASHINGTON, D. C.

AJAX RUBBER CO., INC.
MILLBROOK, N. Y.

SIVAD

M. DAVIS & SONS CO.
NEW YORK

BBS

BEACON BOOK SHOP
NEW YORK

NATIONAL SCVLPTVRE SOCIETY

NATIONAL
SCULPTURE SOCIETY
NEW YORK

COMMUNITY CHEST OF SAN FRANCISCO

COMMUNITY
CHEST OF SAN FRANCISCO
SAN FRANCISCO

CHAMPION COATED PAPER CO.
NEW YORK

39

TICONDEROGA PULP & PAPER CO.
TICONDEROGA, N. Y.

NATIONAL ORGANIZATION FOR
PUBLIC HEALTH NURSING
NEW YORK

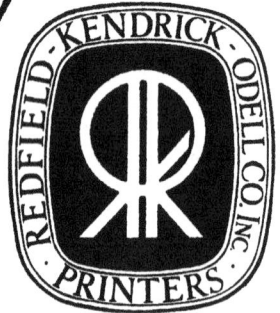

CAMMEYER
NEW YORK

REDFIELD-KENDRICK-ODELL CO.
NEW YORK

THE CURTIS PUBLISHING COMPANY
THE COUNTRY GENTLEMAN
PHILADELPHIA

MINTON, BALCH & CO.
NEW YORK

FRANKLIN AUTOMOBILE COMPANY
SYRACUSE

STEVENS-DURYEA, INC.
CHICOPEE FALLS, MASS.

THE SPIRIT OF YOUTH
IN YOUR FEET

GROUND GRIPPER SHOE CO., INC.
EAST LYNN, MASS.

WINDMILL

GEO. BORGFELDT & CO.
NEW YORK

GOOD

GRAFFIN & DOLSON
NEW YORK

HARTFORD ACCIDENT & INDEMNITY COMPANY
HARTFORD

LOON

JAMES SCARLETT
SEATTLE

FOWLER & UNION HORSE NAIL CO.
NEW HAVEN

WAHTONAH
A CAMP FOR GIRLS
CAPE COD BAY

RODGERS HOSIERY CO., INC.
PHILADELPHIA

THE EUGENE McGUCKIN CO.
PHILADELPHIA

HERMAN G. POHLMAN
CHICAGO

THE ROOKWOOD
POTTERY COMPANY
CINCINNATI

THE NINETEEN HUNDRED WASHER CO.
BINGHAMTON, N.Y.

KENWOOD

WOOL PRODUCTS

F. C. HUYCK & SONS
ALBANY, N.Y.

CALOL

STANDARD OIL COMPANY (CALIFORNIA)
SAN FRANCISCO

THE TEXAS COMPANY
NEW YORK

P P C

PUBLISHERS PRINTING CO.
NEW YORK

MICHAELS STERN
Value First Clothes

MICHAELS STERN & CO.
ROCHESTER

SWP

COVER THE EARTH

ATLANTIC OCEAN
AFRICA EUROPE

THE SHERWIN-WILLIAMS CO.
CLEVELAND

OZMO OIL REFINING CO.
SAN FRANCISCO

43

THE AMERICAN-SCANDINAVIAN
FOUNDATION
NEW YORK

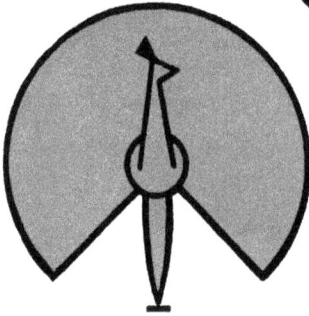

PFAU'S AMERICAN INSTRUMENTS CO.
NEW YORK

THE DE KLYN CANDY CO.
CLEVELAND

ROBERT·L·STILLSON
COMPANY·NEW YORK

ROBERT L. STILLSON COMPANY
NEW YORK

AMERICAN CHAIN COMPANY, INC.
BRIDGEPORT, CONN.

J. W. ONEAL CHEMICAL CO.
ADENA, OHIO

THE WALKER ENGRAVING CO.
NEW YORK

44

STANDARD OIL COMPANY (CALIFORNIA)
SAN FRANCISCO

JORDAN MOTOR
CAR COMPANY, INC.
CLEVELAND

THE PARAFFINE
COMPANIES INC.
SAN FRANCISCO

DUPONT MOTORS INC.
WILMINGTON, DEL.

WESTINGHOUSE
ELECTRIC & MANUFACTURING COMPANY
NEW YORK

AMERICAN TRANSOCEANIC TRADERS CO.
NEW YORK

THE ATCHISON,
TOPEKA & SANTA FE RAILWAY CO.
CHICAGO

WM. ANDERSON TEXTILE MFG. CO., INC.
NEW YORK

DITTO, INCORPORATED
CHICAGO

TRAUB MANUFACTURING CO.
DETROIT

THE NAIRN LINOLEUM COMPANY
KEARNY, N.J.

GRISWOLD

H. J. HEINZ CO.
PITTSBURGH

THE GRISWOLD MANUFACTURING CO.
ERIE, PA.

Snowman
SUGAR

FOUNDED IN 1728 BY BENJAMIN FRANKLIN

UNION SUGAR CO.
SAN FRANCISCO

BEAVER
B·P·Co

FRANKLIN PRINTING COMPANY
PHILADELPHIA

M and F

THE BEAVER PRODUCTS
COMPANY, INC.
BUFFALO

M. & F. SCHLOSSER
NEW YORK

47

BOMBAY BLACK

THE GLIDDEN COMPANY
CLEVELAND

HELBURN THOMPSON COMPANY
SALEM, MASS.

W.IRVING

W. IRVING FORGE INC.
NEW YORK

THE MINNEAPOLIS JOURNAL
MINNEAPOLIS

A. A. WIRE COMPANY
NEWARK

THE ROGER WILLIAMS COMPANY
CLEVELAND

48

STANFORD BRIGGS INC.
NEW YORK

P. F. VOLLAND COMPANY
CHICAGO

NORTHERN PACIFIC RAILWAY CO.
ST. PAUL

FARMERS' COMMISSION HOUSE, INC.
NEW YORK

THE J. C. HUB MANUFACTURING CO.
CLEVELAND

BEAVER STATE FURNITURE CO.
PORTLAND

COLUMBIA PHONOGRAPH COMPANY, INC.
NEW YORK

LEE TIRE & RUBBER CO.
NEW YORK

WILLIAM LYLE COOK
SAN FRANCISCO

GEORGE H. DORAN COMPANY
NEW YORK

THE OHIO STEEL FOUNDRY COMPANY
LIMA, OHIO

MONMOUTH CT. FARMERS' EXCHANGE
FREEHOLD, N.J.

DOVE ❀ MILL

Geo.W.
Wheelwright
Paper Co.

BRISTOLS

GEORGE W. WHEELWRIGHT PAPER CO.
NEW YORK

DELPARK

DELPARK INC.
NEW YORK

T

TAPPAN

TAPPAN STOVE CO.
MANSFIELD, OHIO

D

SQUARE D COMPANY
DETROIT

LEWIS J. ROBER
MINNEAPOLIS

TYPOGRAPHERS
JB
CHICAGO

J. M. BUNDSCHO INC.
CHICAGO

CO-OPERATIVE LEAGUE OF THE
UNITED STATES OF AMERICA,
ASSOCIATION, INC.
NEW YORK

51

AUGUST BECKER
NEW YORK

B. KUPPENHEIMER & CO. INC.
CHICAGO

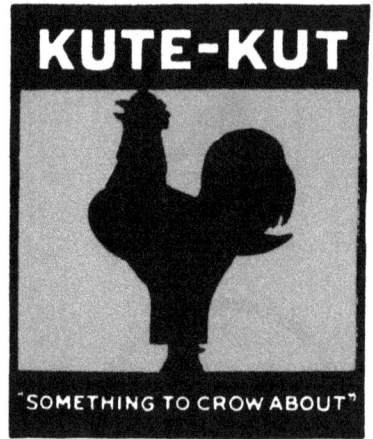

KUTE-KUT
"SOMETHING TO CROW ABOUT"

ELOESSER-HEYNEMANN CO.
SAN FRANCISCO

DOUBLEDAY, PAGE & CO.
GARDEN CITY, N.Y.

LIFE EXTENSION INSTITUTE
NEW YORK

THE ATLANTIC MONTHLY COMPANY
BOSTON

NEENAH PAPER COMPANY
NEENAH, WIS.

PLYMOUTH CORDAGE CO.
NORTH PLYMOUTH, MASS.

ALEXANDER HAMILTON INSTITUTE
NEW YORK

FREDERICK A. STOKES COMPANY
NEW YORK

MAC MANUS
INCORPORATED
DETROIT

THE SPRECKELS SAVAGE TIRE CO.
SAN DIEGO, CAL.

THE ART STUDENTS
LEAGUE OF NEW YORK
NEW YORK

TROJALENE OIL CO.
SAN FRANCISCO

THE GOLDSCHMIDT CORPORATION
NEW YORK

THE NATIONAL SHAWMUT BANK
BOSTON

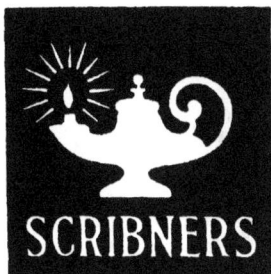

CHAS. SCRIBNER'S SONS
NEW YORK

NIPPON TEA CO.
CLEVELAND

FULLER & SMITH
CLEVELAND

FAWCETT & FAWCETT
NEW YORK

CRANE & CO., INC.
DALTON, MASS.

HARCOURT, BRACE AND COMPANY
NEW YORK

MARBURG BROS., INC.
NEW YORK

THE DIMOCK ORCHARD

JULIAN A. DIMOCK
EAST CORINTH, VT.

Avona

JORDAN MARSH COMPANY
BOSTON

GREEN GATE INN

GREEN GATE INN
SAN FRANCISCO

AMERICAN TELEPHONE & TELEGRAPH CO.
BELL SYSTEM
AND ASSOCIATED COMPANIES

AMERICAN TELEPHONE
AND TELEGRAPH COMPANY
NEW YORK

NATIONAL

NATIONAL BLANK BOOK CO.
LOCKPORT, N.Y.

G

THE B. F. GOODRICH
RUBBER CO.
AKRON

SALOMON & WIENER INC.
NEW YORK

E. WEYHE
NEW YORK

TOVT·BIEN·OV·RIEN

HOUGHTON MIFFLIN COMPANY
BOSTON

NON·REFERT
BONOS·HABEAS QVAM·MVLTOS
L·B·&·C°
QVAM·SED·QVAM

LITTLE, BROWN, AND COMPANY
BOSTON

ABCD
EFGH
IJKL
MNO&

THE ATHENÆUM PRESS

GINN AND COMPANY
CAMBRIDGE, MASS.

STORK

THE STORK CO.
NEW YORK

SKOOKUM PACKERS ASSN., INC.
WENATCHEE, WASH.

WESTERN
TOBACCO CO., INC.
NEW YORK

STATE OF MAINE PUBLICITY BUREAU
PORTLAND, ME.

HAWKES

T. G. HAWKES & CO.
CORNING, N.Y.

BRAW LADDIE GOLF CO.
OAKLAND

BLACK SWAN PHONOGRAPH CO.
NEW YORK

DENVER GAS &
ELECTRIC LIGHT CO.
DENVER

LIBERTY PAPER CO.
NEW YORK

SI-MONDS SAW AND
STEEL CO.
FITCHBURG, MASS.

DIVISION OF PICTORIAL PUBLICITY
WASHINGTON, D.C.

GIANT UMBRELLA CO.
NEW YORK

MORTON SALT CO.
CHICAGO

THE THEROZ COMPANY
NEW YORK

MULHOLLAND BROS., INC.
AURORA, ILL.

HESS MANUFACTURING CO
PHILADELPHIA

TRADE MARK

G. E. BURSLEY & COMPANY
FORT WAYNE, IND.

THE BECK ENGRAVING COMPANY
NEW YORK

EASTCO

EASTERN MANUFACTURING
COMPANY
NEW YORK

CAMEL

ASHTABULA CORRUGATED BOX CO.
ASHTABULA, OHIO

1850
1922

L. L. BROWN PAPER
COMPANY
ADAMS, MASS.

60

ΛΑΜΠΑΔΙΑ ΕΧΟΝΤΕΣ ΔΙΑΔΩΣΟΥΣΙΝ ΑΛΛΗΛΟΙΣ

HARPER & BROTHERS
NEW YORK

H. LOEB & COMPANY
NEW YORK

TRUTH WELL TOLD

THE H. K. McCANN COMPANY
NEW YORK

THE AMERICAN INSTITUTE OF GRAPHIC ARTS
NEW YORK

THE AXIS OF THE BUSINESS WORLD

A. W. SHAW COMPANY
CHICAGO

CAVALIER FURNITURE

TENNESSEE FURNITURE CORP.
CHATTANOOGA, TENN.

DARD HUNTER
CHILLICOTHE, OHIO

GLEN BUCK
CHICAGO

THE ARMAND COMPANY, INC.
DES MOINES, IOWA

CUTLER MAIL CHUTE COMPANY
ROCHESTER

SALMAGUNDI CLUB
NEW YORK

THE FIRM OF BEED
NEW YORK

ST. LAWRENCE BOAT WORKS, INC.
OGDENSBURG, N.Y.

62

INDEX

63

www.ingramcontent.com/pod-product-compliance
Lightning Source LLC
Chambersburg PA
CBHW051338200326
41519CB00026B/7477